D1712120

KOTERBA—

Drawing You In

For my mom

Contents

2 Foreword

4 Introduction

16 It Starts With an Idea

30 Sketching Toward a Concept

40 It's OK to Make a Mess

52 In Search of Some Appeal

66 When Words Come First

76 If Only They All Could Be Easy

86 Making an Unexpected Connection

96 From Omaha to Orbit

110 A Techie Come Lately

120 Cold With a Chance of Sketches

126 Scoring Points With Readers

138 In Remembrance

148 A Slice of Everyday Life

162 All the President's Features

170 A Few More Lines

188 Acknowledgments

189 About Jeff Koterba

I F YOU THINK there's nothing as powerful as the written word, put this book down. Walk away. Quickly. I warn you because as a lover of language, compelling writing and the artfully crafted phrase, as someone who has spent a career at the keyboard, I always believed that one word was worth a thousand pictures.

Then I met Jeff Koterba. As The World-Herald's editorial cartoonist for the past 25 years, Jeff has created pictures with a point. Whatever the issue of the day — whether it's potholes in our streets or the tax man's hand in your pocket — his drawings have impact. They make you nod in agreement. They make you shake your head in disgust.

A long-winded Washington columnist can take a thousand words to point out the difficulties of bringing Western-style democracy to the Middle East. Jeff can do it with one drawing of the Sphinx wearing a saddle. That's why the 19th-century New York political scoundrel William "Boss" Tweed once said, "I don't care what the papers write about me. My constituents can't read. But damn it, they can see the pictures."

See the pictures, think about an issue. That's the hope for each drawing.

Jeff is a lifelong Omahan with a global perspective. His subjects range from Rosenblatt Stadium to outer space. After a cartoon appears, readers sometimes call and demand that Jeff be fired. Others call and sing his praises. But most often, his cartoon will make us laugh. Even if you disagree with the way he sees something, it's hard not to chuckle when Jeff puts pen to paper.

And funnily enough, good humor is often the reaction a cartoon will bring from its subject. Time after time — once they've cussed him, his editor and his newspaper — a politician or other person who's just been jabbed by the Koterba pen will call and ask if, please, would it be possible for Jeff to provide the original?

His artwork hangs framed on office walls from City Hall to the Unicameral to the nation's Capitol. So, word lovers, you've been warned. Turn the page now and you will meet Jeff Koterba. You'll nod, you'll cuss, you'll laugh. You'll see the power of a picture.

There's still time to turn away. But that would be a mistake.

Michael Holmes
Editorial Page Editor

Thumbnail Sketches and Ink on My Fingers

WHEN I WAS GROWING UP in the 1960s, my father, Art, repaired broken TVs and resold them from our front porch in South Omaha by advertising in the classifieds of the Sunday World-Herald. On Saturday evenings, he often would drive downtown in our Buick to pick up the early edition of the next day's paper. Never mind that we subscribed to The World-Herald and would receive the Sunday paper early the next morning — he liked seeing his ad in print as soon as the paper came off the presses, when you could still smell the ink drying. For my father, I think there was something "official" about his ad appearing in The World-Herald. The newspaper gave his ad a certain prestige.

I often accompanied my father on these journeys. The excitement for me was getting the chance to glimpse the Sunday funnies on Saturday. Reading Peanuts and the Wizard of Id the night before other kids did made me feel like a time traveler holding the key to some great secret.

For as long as I can remember, I've loved to draw, and on those Saturday nights I would sneak off to my room with the Sunday comic section and attempt to re-create what I saw in print. Except that my father didn't approve of copying.

Be unique, he preached. So I came up with my own characters. Dogie the Doggie, for example, was my answer to Snoopy, my way of showing my father that I was capable of being original.

My mother also inspired me with little drawings and puzzles that she left under my pillow in an envelope — like the cartoon fairy. She often would sit patiently as we went through a step-by-step drawing book we had picked up at a garage sale, attempting to re-create what we saw in its pages. Her drawing of a steam locomotive coming around the bend, her perspective, the grain elevators in the background, were precise and beautiful. If only I could draw like that, I would say, and she would assure me that one day I would, and better.

At around the age of 7, I "founded" my own newspaper, The Dogie The Doggie News, which usually included a front-page story of "news" — a tornado ripping apart South Omaha, for example. Otherwise, it was filled with cartoons, mostly about my hero, Dogie (rhymes with bogey). I guess you could say it was more tabloid than anything resembling a real newspaper. Still, I would parade around our house, calling out "Extra! Extra!" until eventually my parents would spring for the 10 cents I would charge for that day's one and only hand-drawn edition.

Drawing of Dogie, circa 1968

Eventually, I became a newspaper carrier and felt pride walking through my neighborhood, The World-Herald logo emblazoned on my carrier bag.

I would glance at the headlines as I folded the paper for delivery. And as I got older, my reading of the World-Herald expanded beyond the comics to the sports and news pages, and eventually the editorial page.

The cartoons on the editorial pages were populated not with dogs and wizards but with local, national and world leaders.

The legendary Hank Barrow — who had come to The World-Herald from New York — was the first editorial cartoonist I recall.

Always Happens the Morning After

CUBAN PROPAGANDA

ED FISCHER ©.'75
©OMAHA WORLD-HERALD
DISTRIBUTED BY McNAUGHT SYNDICATE

I never met Barrow but always appreciated his old-school drafts-manship, his use of shadow and contrast. His drawings were filled with undertones of graveness.

Ed Fischer followed. I loved the looseness of his lines, his sense of whimsy and humor in his ideas and how his cartoons managed to skewer newsmakers in a devilish and delicious way. But you got the sense from his cartoons that he didn't hate anyone, he was merely pointing out their foibles and hypocrisies in a Midwestern way. His work was inviting and good-natured. And yet somehow it had bite.

Throughout grade school I continued to draw and often sketched into the night, because my heart told me I was meant to do something with art. At Omaha South High School, I drew cartoons for the school newspaper, the Tooter. I also worked in The World-Herald's dispatch department as a "tearsheet clerk," ripping pages from the early edition to give advertisers proof that their ad had made it into print.

During my senior year, Fischer conducted a cartoon contest, and I submitted a drawing of Uncle Sam juggling eggs — labeled with hot-button issues the United States faced at the time.
The contest winners were to be printed on the op-ed page a few Sundays later, and the night before I went downtown once again with my father to pick up an early edition. I paged through the newspaper as we drove down 13th Street on the way home, the streetlights fading in and out as we passed them in the car. At last I reached the op-ed page, only to find that my cartoon hadn't made the cut.

I was devastated. A few days later, however, the phone rang before I left for school.
My father answered and said, "It's for you. It's Ed Fischer."

"Hello, Ed Fischer!" I remember saying loudly into the receiver, practically hyperventilating. Fischer explained that he had chosen me as one of the winners but that the lines of my drawing were too thin to reproduce in the newspaper. "I even tried to thicken up your lines," he said. "But I couldn't get it to work."

That Fischer, my cartooning hero, not only would call me but attempt to improve my drawing was one of the great moments in my life. I soon met him, and he took me under his wing, helping to develop my drawings and ideas. One of the most profound things he said to me was that cartooning was a "calling."

That was exactly as I had always felt, but now someone had given it a name. I went on to draw cartoons for the University of Nebraska at Omaha's Gateway and spent nearly a decade freelancing. By then, Fischer had departed to his home state of Minnesota, leaving The World-Herald's cartooning job vacant. For several years I sent my work to the editor at the time, Frank Partsch, who was kind and encouraging and purchased a few freelance cartoons from me. But I couldn't get hired, and the truth is, I wasn't ready for the job. I lacked experience on deadline and needed more time to develop my ideas and drawing style.

So as I had since childhood, I would work into the night attempting to perfect my craft. And to prove to Frank I could do the job.

Then the worst thing happened. The World-Herald offered the job to Steve Kelley, who was not only an excellent cartoonist but also a stand-up comedian. But on the day he was to fly to Omaha to take the job, the San Diego Union called and hired him. As he would later tell Jay Leno on "The Tonight Show," he had a choice to make between Omaha and San Diego, "so I flipped a coin. The coin came up Omaha. So I flipped again. San Diego won best out of seven."

Luckily for me. Not long after a few trial-and-error freelancing efforts for The World-Herald, Frank offered me the job — which had been vacant for nine years — on a "trial basis." I wept in his office.

A few days later, reality hit. How would I be able to draw a cartoon six days a week? How many was that in a year? In a — gulp — career? I was afraid to do the math. Frank reassured me that the entirety of a journalist's work isn't made in one day. Indeed, you can only take it one day at a time. He would become my greatest mentor, helping me not just with concepts and art but also — and just as important — with my word choices.

Another Ed played a significant role in developing my "voice" as a cartoonist. I never met Ed Koterba, my father's brother, but I got to know him through my father's stories of his travels around the globe as a reporter and columnist. Uncle Ed got his start with The World-Herald in the 1930s and eventually became a syndicated columnist for Scripps Howard and a member of the White House press corps during the Kennedy administration. He interviewed the likes of rocket pioneer Wernher von Braun and covered the early days of the U.S. space program. Uncle Ed was killed in a plane crash just weeks after I was born. President Kennedy began a press conference by eulogizing him — something I witnessed in adulthood, thanks to video footage from the John F. Kennedy Library.

Still, I felt like I knew Uncle Ed — at least the journalist part of him — through his columns, which showed his good-natured spirit, economy of words and fairness. And from the amazing stories he covered from the Soviet Union, from first-person accounts of his visiting his parents' homeland in Czechoslovakia and from his attempts at becoming one of the first journalists to land by plane at the South Pole.

If you had to label Uncle Ed's politics, it would be centrist. And though I wasn't politically aware when I started reading Ed Fischer's editorial cartoons, I realized later that Fischer also took shots at both sides of the aisle — no one seemed immune from his pen.

My parents also had that centrist streak in them. Besides fixing TVs, my father was a drummer and a union man with the Omaha Musicians Association for just under 72 years. I often heard him complain about high taxes. And while he might have criticized politicians on either end of the spectrum, he did so in a good-natured way. My mother was well-informed and often attended Omaha school board meetings. Both parents voted in every election but always held their choices close to the vest. I've never known my mother's political affiliation. And until after his death in 2013, I honestly didn't know that my father had been a lifelong Democrat.

Other voices also influenced me. Long before I came along, my father played drums for Johnny Carson when he was still a traveling magician and always had a special fondness for Johnny. Because of that connection, so did I. And with all those extra TVs around our house (and a very late bedtime), how could I not watch The Tonight Show? Those Carson monologues — filled with jokes about politicians on both sides of the aisle — provided my first tastes of satire on current events. Johnny, it seemed to me, didn't hate anyone. Sure, he was mischievous and irreverent, but there was a warmth I don't often sense from many of the current lineup of talk-show hosts and political comedians.

So I hope my ideas come from a good place — even when I'm being critical. I don't hate anyone, but I might dislike some of their words and actions. I shy away from meeting politicians, because there's always the danger that I might find them charming and likable and want to hold back. In the end, criticism is deserved at times, and points need to be made. That's my job.

Over the years I've had people tell me that I have no business drawing cartoons. That I'm dumb, that I can't draw. A cartoon of President Barack Obama ducking a series of hot-button questions, labeled "Duck Dynasty," gets me called an "extreme right-winger." A cartoon of President George W. Bush confusing the Ten Commandments with the U.S. Constitution is called an example of "left-wing media" bias.

When receiving feedback (read hate mail), I consider what is being said and don't mind constructive criticism. Even when a letter or email is laced with vulgar language, I try to read beyond it, to understand why someone is upset. A reader once told me: I can't tell if you're a mean asshole or just a stupid asshole. I was shocked, of course, but when I read on, I understood where she was coming from. Truth be told, if I had to do it again, I might have drawn that cartoon differently.

In this world of red vs. blue, right vs. left, I sense that many of us are exhausted from shouting matches on cable news programs. And while "moderate" doesn't sound sexy, for me as a cartoonist, it makes the most sense. The middle gives me the opportunity to offer a third or fourth angle on an issue. And for the record: I'm not out to change anyone's mind. Mostly, I'm hoping simply to drop in on the conversation and give my two cents' worth (the penny is still in circulation, isn't it?), and then, just as quickly, duck out.

I've grown to know my audience's likes and dislikes. Maybe it's because I was born and raised in Nebraska and have breathed the air, felt the Midwestern cold on my face. Maybe it's because I know Dodge Street like the decades-old ink blots on my drawing table. All my life I've had a strong connection with my mom. I can't tell you how many times I knew the phone was going to ring, and it would be her. And vice versa. I hope to have developed a little bit of that same relationship with my readers. Who are, to me, like family.

There aren't many full-time newspaper cartoonists left, but The World-Herald carries on a strong tradition. I'm only the fifth full-time cartoonist in the newspaper's history and have been drawing for 25 years. It's occurred to me only in recent years that no one officially said that I'd passed the trial basis. And maybe that's how it should be. You're only as good as your latest cartoon. And tomorrow, there's always another deadline, and another opportunity to try harder. …

It Starts With an Idea

I'M NOT OUT TO deliberately anger anyone. My goal is to draw compelling cartoons based on the truth as I see it. But first, I need ideas. I honestly don't know how they come to me, but I can tell you how to prepare a landing strip for their arrival: read, read, read.

I start with The World-Herald and many other newspapers. No other form of news gathering gives me the depth I need for a good cartoon idea, and I'm not just saying this because I'm in the business of print and online journalism. I simply like to dig beyond the headlines for ideas to sink my teeth into. But I occasionally take a look at TV news — from all perspectives — and blogs. And radio news, magazines and books, both fiction and nonfiction.

I also try to give myself some quiet time to think. Sometimes it takes me hours to come up with an idea, but other times, boom! Just like that, the idea presents itself.

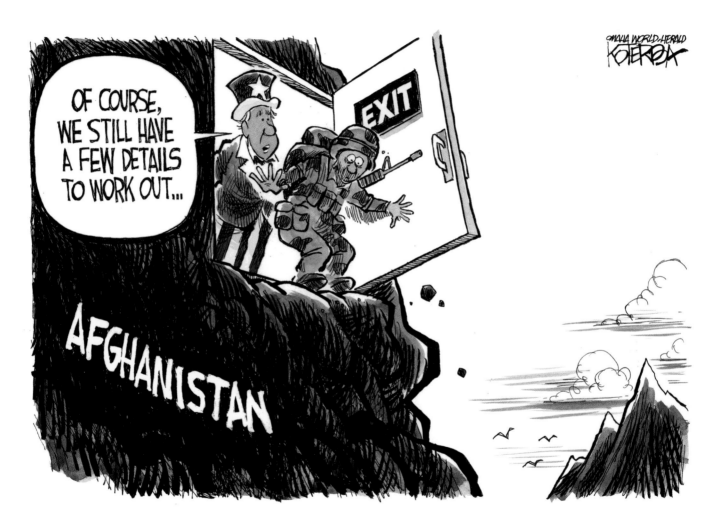

KOTERBA
OMAHA WORLD-HERALD

POLITICAL VENTRILOQUISM...

NEGATIVE ADS

SECRET DONORS

OMAHA WORLD-HERALD KOTERBA

PHOTO FINISH

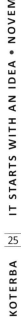

Sketching Toward a Concept

IN THE MORNING, I search for inspiration while sketching, sometimes thumbnails on scraps of paper or little drawings on receipts. I hope the day's idea comes easily, like a flash of lightning. (I should know, since I've been hit by lightning. But that's a story for later.)

But most of the time, it's a matter of a couple of decent starting points. When I settle on one to pursue, I get the approval of my editor, Mike Holmes. He'll challenge me when he needs to, but he also sometimes grants me the best compliment a cartoonist can receive: a heartfelt laugh.

Most of the time, I can address any concerns with a revised sketch, but sometimes the idea is just shot down. Maybe because I'm missing some insight on the topic, or perhaps the thought just isn't working. As gloomy as a rejection leaves me, I'll usually understand the concerns that are raised. But on occasion, I don't agree, and that's OK, too. If the cartoonist and the editor were always in lockstep, where would we find the creative tension?

However the idea makes it to my drawing table, my goal each day is to have a solid concept by lunchtime. Otherwise, I'll find myself munching on a sandwich, with lettuce and tomato falling onto my sketches. Or skipping lunch altogether.

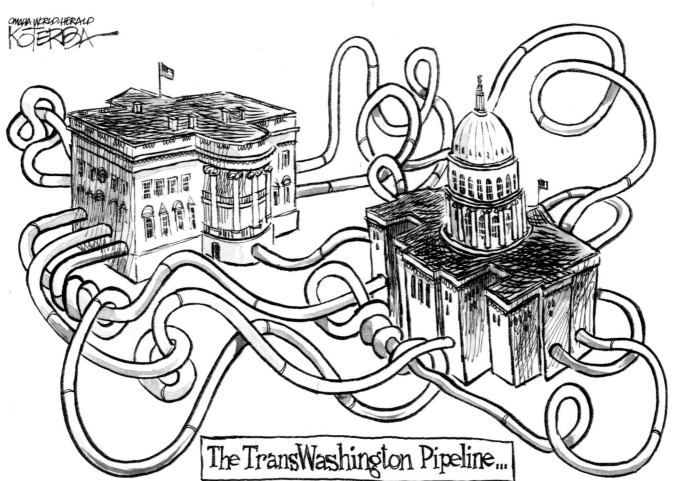

The TransWashington Pipeline...

NEBRASKA CHILD SAFETY NET

A PORTRAIT OF SENATOR CHAMBERS

Eisenhower Kennedy Johnson Nixon Ford Carter Reagan Bush Clinton Bush

OMAHA WORLD-HERALD 2001
JEFF KOTERBA

It's OK to Make a Mess

I'D LIKE TO THINK THE QUALITY of my drawings has improved after 25 years at The World-Herald. When I first landed the job, I got it into my head that I needed to give my editor as many lines as possible. Which meant really busy and wordy drawings, or so it seems as I look back now on my early work. Over the years, I've allowed more white space and fewer words to enter the sacred space of the drawings, giving the cartoon more room to breathe.

My tools of the trade have remained basically the same. I still make rough sketches in pencil and then redraw each cartoon on a sheet of Bristol board. Next, I ink in the lines using an assortment of pens and brushes. But here's what has changed: For a good portion of my career, my finished cartoons appeared only in black and white. In 2007, I began adding color. After finishing the black and white version, I'll make a copy on another sheet of Bristol and hand paint that version, in essence creating two "originals."

Most cartoonists work in Photoshop or another software program. Nothing wrong with that, I appreciate technology as much as the next cartoonist. A cartoonist friend once asked me which "software program" I used to paint my cartoons. When I told him, "watercolor," he said, "Oh, which watercolor software program?" It took a few minutes for me to explain that I was using actual watercolor.

He seemed disturbed by my response. "What happens if you make a mistake? You don't have an 'undo' button."

"Nope," I said. "If I mess up, I just make another copy and start again."

He shook his head. "We need to get you using your computer to color in your cartoons."

I still haven't done it. Not to say that I won't one day — and not to say that I haven't on occasion tweaked my work using Photoshop (for example, it's much easier to hand-letter words in black and then switch them to color in Photoshop).

But I love the tactile experience of hand-painting and of going home each night with ink and paint on my fingers. Plus, I prefer the look of something hand-painted, the naturalness of it, even when something unexpected happens — when colors bleed together in a strange way or a smudge of color appears where it shouldn't.

My son, Josh, taught me a Japanese term: wabisabi. It's the acceptance and appreciation of the beauty of the imperfect. I'm not perfect, far from it. There's also an imperfection that comes with art created by hand. To my eye, it's more human, so it's more beautiful.

And after all, life is messy. Politics, especially.

'GO TO SLEEP, DEAR... YOU'RE JUST PARANOID.'

In Search of Some Appeal

I TRY TO MIX UP the topics, balancing what I'm seeing in the news — the "big" story — with what might simply catch readers' interest. Same for tone. If I've been drawing on lots of dark, depressing and heavy topics, I'll try to lighten the mood. If I'm feeling overwhelmed by depressing issues, my guess is that the reader is, too.

But big story or small, weighty or lighthearted, my priority is always the local cartoon. When I draw about mayors or governors, I'm fairly certain they will read my work the next day. I can't always say that's the case for national and international newsmakers, although I do occasionally hear from them as well. Mostly, though, I enjoy drawing about the people and issues that directly affect our readers.

I keep my ear to the ground and use this formula when deciding what to draw:

1. What's making news today?

2. What will be in the news tomorrow?

3. How does this topic impact World-Herald readers?

4. Have I drawn on too many serious topics lately or not enough?

5. Do I have anything new and interesting to say on the topic?

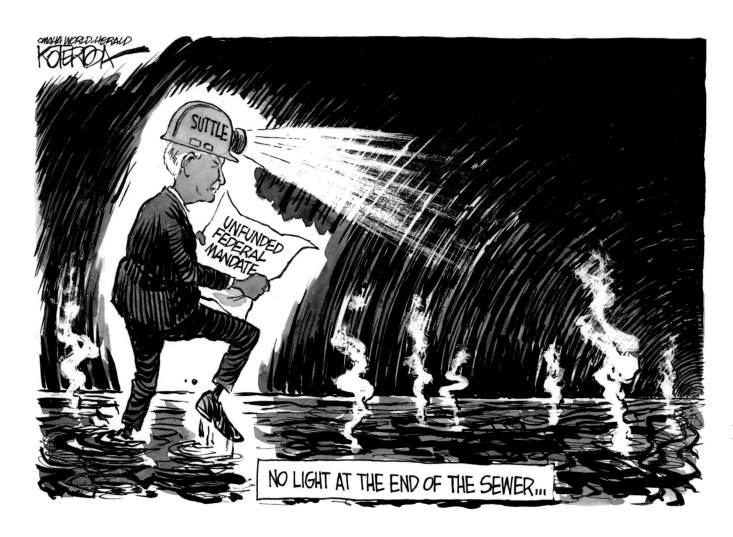

I WANT (FEWER OF) YOU

OMAHA WORLD-HERALD
KOTERBA

TAXPAYER
CONVENTION CENTER AND ARENA

NAMING RIGHTS

READY... AIM...

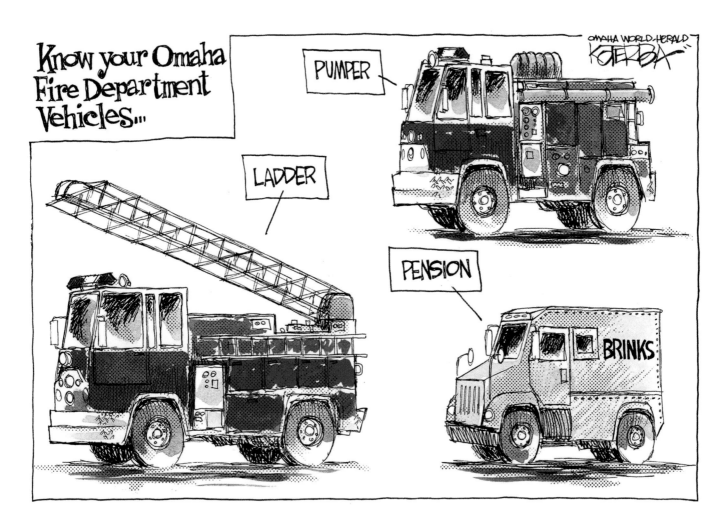

Know your Omaha Fire Department Vehicles...

PUMPER

LADDER

PENSION

BRINKS

OMAHA WORLD-HERALD KOTERBA

When Words Come First

WHEN A BUDDING CARTOONIST asks how to pursue the profession, I say you must draw every day. You must stay up late, forgo sleep, squirrel away chunks of time and fill up sketchbook after sketchbook. But I'm quick to follow that advice with this: You must also read, read, read. Because when you're creating a painting, a sculpture or a cartoon, you need meat behind it or even the most skilled artwork will come off as empty. In fact, I'd rather read a cartoon with a marginal drawing and a great idea than the opposite. Of course, when you can hit on all cylinders, all the better.

Over the years I hope that, like my drawings, I also have improved my writing. My earlier cartoons were a lot busier, I think. Part of that was because I felt so grateful to have the job that I wanted to give my employer as much detail in my drawings as possible. And all too often, as many words. But over the years, I also began taking my writing more seriously and realized the importance of the word part of the cartoon.

My editors and colleagues on the editorial page have helped immensely. Loved ones, too, have offered their opinions — when I've asked. They've all challenged me, reminding me that in a cartoon, every word is on trial for its life.

"WE FINALLY GOT BIN LADEN, DADDY..."

WE HAVE MET THE HERO AND HE IS US

FROM OUT OF NOWHERE,
LIKE A CHILL IN THE NIGHT,
HE LEAKED SECRETS LONG HELD,
BY LIPS CLOSED SO TIGHT.

HE CRIED OUT: "FLASH DRIVES,
FLASH DRIVES FOR ALL!
THEY KNOW WHEN YOU SURF
THEY KNOW WHEN YOU CALL!"

BUT SOON HE WAS GONE,
DECLARING HE'D "WON."
HE RETURNED TO THE SNOW,
HIS WORK HERE WAS "DONE."

SOME CALLED HIM A TRAITOR,
OTHERS SAID HE'D DONE WELL.
SECURITY OR PRIVACY?
ONLY HISTORY WILL TELL.

KOTERBA
OMAHA WORLD-HERALD

DEPRIVED OF SLEEP FOR YEARS, NED FLICKESWORTH WAS CONVINCED THERE
HAD TO BE A GOVERNMENT PROGRAM TO REIMBURSE HIM FOR HIS LOST HOURS OF SHUT-EYE

If Only They All Could Be Easy

Some days I have the easiest job in the world. I get up in the morning, pick up the paper, immediately see a story that grabs my attention, and voilà, an idea pops into my head. I'll scramble for any scrap of paper — a receipt, a napkin — to jot it down. Maybe I'll email it to myself.

But sometimes I'm suspicious when an idea comes so quickly, so unexpectedly and without much thought. Why? For one, it rarely happens. But also, I know that good ideas take time to ferment. Preparation and study are involved. Reading and research. Sometimes I come across a topic that just isn't ready. Like planting a seed, I hold onto it, allowing my subconscious to do some of the work for me, knowing that it might bear fruit a few days later.

I once read somewhere that the average length of time a reader spends on an editorial cartoon is 7 seconds. That's a painful statistic. Even when the ideas come quickly, the drawings most often take at least a few hours, depending on the complexity of the concept. Still, on those days when the ideas do come quickly, when an idea has already received the stamp of approval from my editor, it's as though elves have come during the night to grant me a gift.

GOVERNMENT STANDSTILL

GITMO

Making an Unexpected Connection

LONGTIME WORLD-HERALD COLUMNIST Mike Kelly has very generously said many nice things about my work. But the best compliment was when he said that he didn't know how I managed to combine two very different topics into one cartoon. Until he said that, I wasn't fully aware that I had. That's just how my brain works: I look for connections in things.

I have Tourette's syndrome, and there is anecdotal evidence that those with Tourette's are creative in some way. I don't often have the Hollywood version of Tourette's where I swear all the time (although sometimes my readers swear at me). Rather, I display strange tics and twitches and make odd sounds in my throat. I like to think that because of the quirky way my neurons fire, I just happen to have a unique way of seeing the world that allows me to make connections between two completely unrelated topics.

ONE DAY, CHINA MAY SURPASS THE U.S. IN SPACE...

MEANWHILE, BACK ON EARTH...

OMAHA WORLD-HERALD
KOTERBA

U.S. TREASURY

"ALL CLEAR...THE PRIMARY IS OVER..."

MAKING AN UNEXPECTED CONNECTION • FEBRUARY 2012

WHEN IT ALL BEGAN...

From Omaha to Orbit

WHEN GROWING UP with all those TVs my father repaired, I was able to watch live coverage of the space program on any number of screens. It was as though we had our own little newsroom. My father told stories of his brother, Uncle Ed, covering the space program and was fascinated with exploring the stars. And along with cartooning and newspapers, a love of space also must have made its way into my bloodstream.

A few months before Neil Armstrong set foot on the moon, I came out with a special edition of The Dogie the Doggie News. The front page announced that Dogie had become the first dog to land on the moon. It wasn't until later that summer that I discovered that a toy manufacturer had already marketed a Snoopy-astronaut doll, declaring that the Peanuts beagle had been first. I was crushed, believing that my Dogie character wasn't as original as I thought.

But my love of space never waned. As a cartoonist, I have often commented on issues related to space exploration and even employed space themes when commenting on non-space issues.

HE GAVE US THE MOON...AND LEFT BEHIND A WORLD OF POSSIBILITIES...

KOTERBA
OMAHA WORLD-HERALD

One morning, I received an email with the subject field: "Greetings, Earthling." At first, I thought the message was spam and nearly deleted it. After opening it, however, I learned that the message was from Clay Anderson, Nebraska's first astronaut. He was writing from the International Space Station to say that my recent cartoon of him had been beamed to the space station.

WELCOME HOME, HUSKERNAUT...

Clay and I kept in touch and eventually met in person on Earth. Later he wrote that he was to return to space on the shuttle Discovery and asked me and my family to attend the launch. He had just one request: Would I be willing to create two original drawings that he could carry on board the space shuttle? Upon his return, one of the drawings would be given to the paper, and the other to me. I was thrilled.

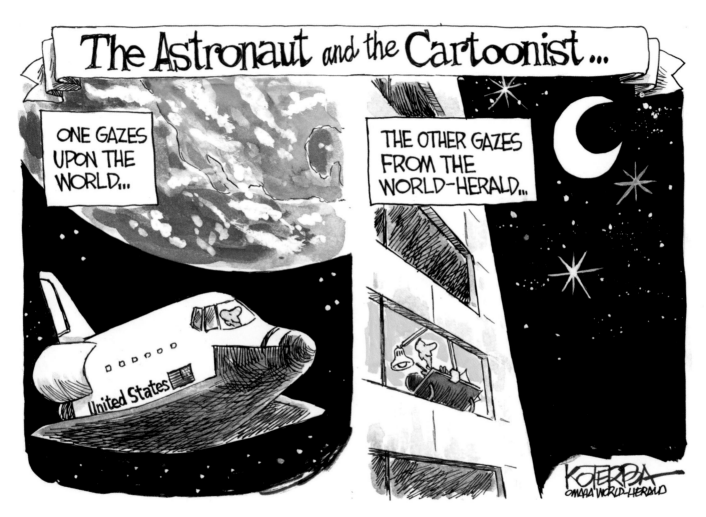

The first idea came easily...

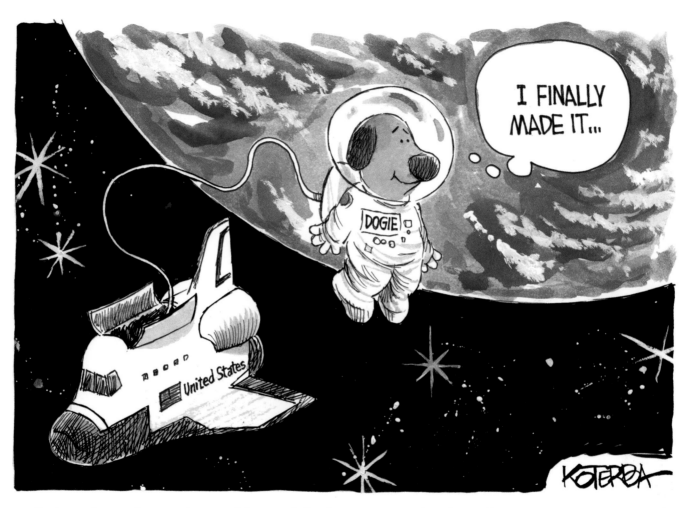

But it was the second cartoon that proved the most challenging. Drawing something for myself seemed strangely self-indulgent.
And then, it came to me…

ENCORE! ENCORE!

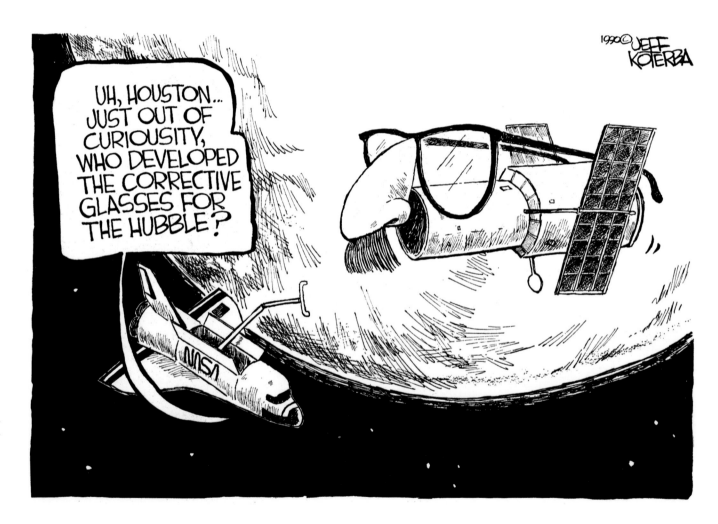

JOHN GLENN IN SPACE...

United States

ASK ME ABOUT MY GRANDKIDS

JEFF KOTERBA 1998
OMAHA WORLD-HERALD

A Techie Come Lately

YOU WOULD THINK I would have taken an early interest in technology, with all those TVs, electronic parts and wires around the house as I was growing up. I did enjoy drawing TVs, but actually figuring out how they work? No thanks.

I was one of the last employees at The World-Herald to use a typewriter. And for a time I was proud of my having avoided using a computer for work. Now, I'm a little shocked at my past self.

My son, Josh, was the one who got me interested in technology. While I still hand draw everything, I enjoy my smartphone, but even more, I love commenting on the latest trends in technology. And if I upgrade my phone, that's research, right?

"KINDLE, NOOK, SONY READER....I SAY, HARDWICK, THIS SURE IS AN IMPRESSIVE LIBRARY."

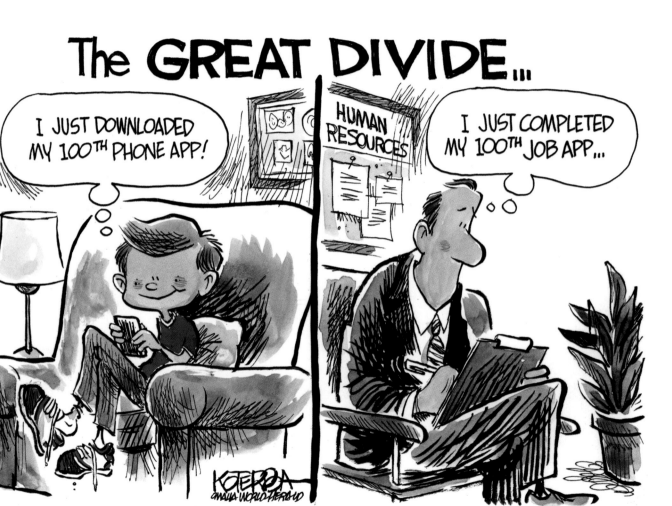

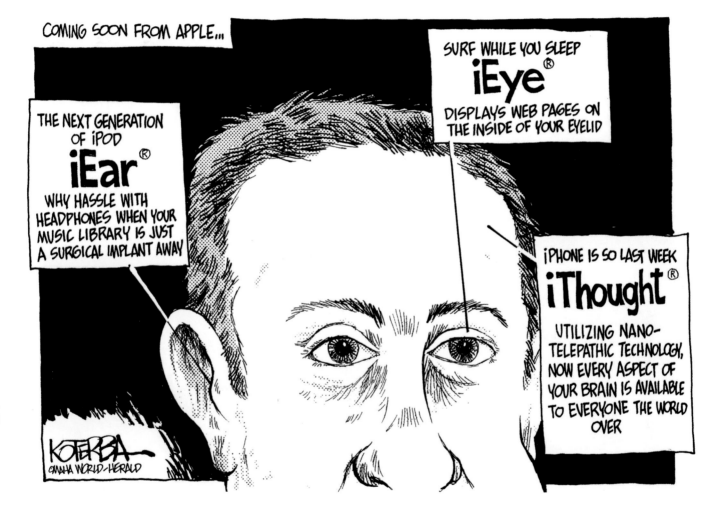

"IT'S NOT THE AMAZON DRONE BRINGING MY PACKAGE THAT CONCERNS ME... IT'S THE NSA DRONE FOLLOWING IT."

"I DON'T KNOW ABOUT YOU, BUT I FEEL WAY BETTER NOW THAT FACEBOOK HAS ADDRESSED OUR CONCERNS ABOUT PRIVACY..."

Cold With a Chance of Sketches

FOR THOSE OF US in the Midlands, weather talk is a pastime. Either it's too cold or too hot, too snowy, or too dry. I learned to follow the weather from my father. Sure, he enjoyed glorious Nebraska autumn days, but mostly he was fascinated with predicting bad weather. I don't know what his secret was, but he often was as accurate, if not more so, than TV weather forecasters.

You'd think I would hate bad weather. First off, there was my 14th birthday, which was the day of the famous May 6, 1975, tornado. Then, between my junior and senior years of high school, I was struck by lightning while watching an approaching storm from my parents' front yard in South Omaha. I thought I was a goner after being knocked to the ground and unable to move for several minutes.

Somehow, I managed to make it into the house, and just a few weeks later, landed my first regular cartooning gig on the high school newspaper. I've been on some type of regular deadline ever since. Even without close encounters with tornadoes and lightning, I'd still be just as interested in weather from a cartooning point of view. Midlanders, even when we can't agree on politics, can almost always find common ground when it comes to the weather.

"REPEAT AFTER ME: AT LEAST WE DON'T GET HURRICANES...
AT LEAST WE DON'T GET HURRICANES...AT LEAST....."

"YES, THE BUGS ARE BAD THIS YEAR...ON THE OTHER HAND,
I'M GETTING A GOOD VIEW OF THE FLOODING."

Scoring Points With Readers

I TRY NOT TO DELVE into sports territory too terribly much — there are just so many other issues to comment on. However, to ignore the pervasiveness of Big Red football — and more recently, the success of the Creighton Bluejays — would be like ignoring Midlands weather.

On the other hand, I tend to think in terms of a baseball player's batting average when pondering my weekly output of cartoons. I figure that if each day I can get on base — whether that's a single, a walk (or even taking a pitch to the body), I'll do what I have to do. And if in the process of drawing I can get a double or maybe even a triple, I figure I'm doing pretty well. And, of course, I strive to hit at least one home run each week.

But I can say without a doubt that a sports cartoon — the one I drew to celebrate 7-year-old cancer patient Jack Hoffman's touchdown run at Nebraska's 2013 spring football game — generated more reader response than anything else I've done.

Nothing but McDermott...

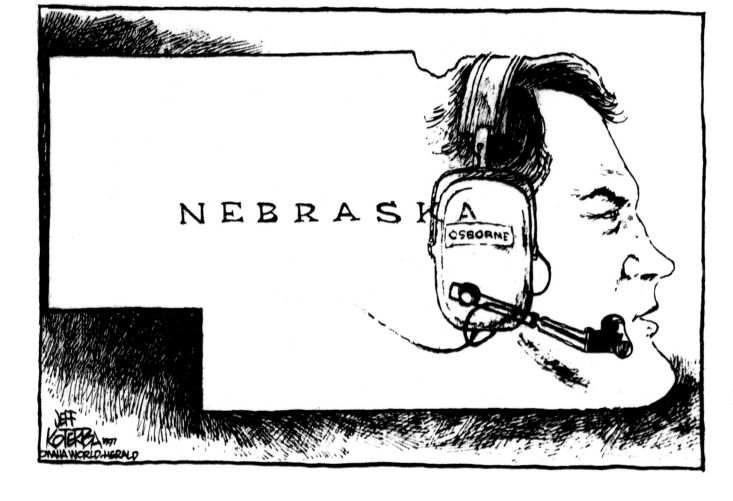

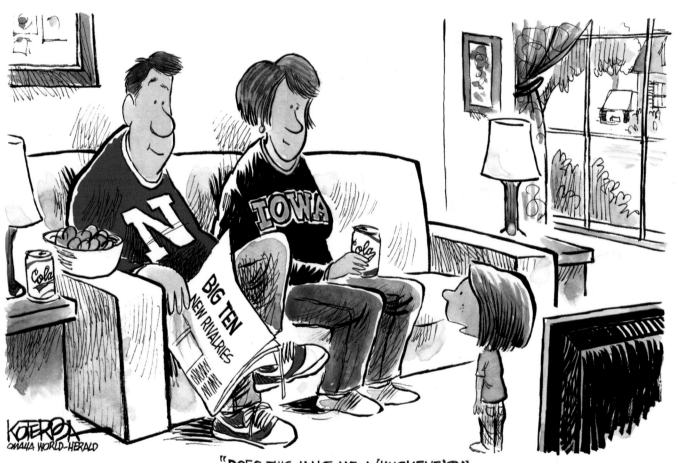

"DOES THIS MAKE ME A 'HUSKEYE'?"

"I THINK THE PRIEST'S MIND IS STILL ON THE GAME...
MY PENANCE IS THREE **OUR FATHERS** AND ONE **HAIL MARY TOUCHDOWN**."

In Remembrance

EARLY IN MY CAREER, I leaned too heavily on the reliable St. Peter and the gates of heaven when drawing a cartoon honoring the passing of a notable person in the news. Clichés are clichés because they work. But somewhere along the way, my father's insistence that I come up with "unique" ideas pushed me to look beyond the obvious.

Why do I memorialize some notable figures who have passed away and not others? Clearly, the passing of some newsmakers is just too big or important to ignore. But others … well, I just follow where the spirit takes me.

THE ROAD TO HEAVEN

JACK DIESING SR.

Sam Mercer.

OMAHA WORLD-HERALD
KOTERBA

THE MAN IN WHITE

MRS. B

A Slice of Everyday Life

SOME DAYS I wake up tired. That is, tired of drawing on too many "heavy" subjects. The Four Horsemen of the Apocalypse, the Big Red losing a big game, that sort of thing.

That's when "Quirky Jeff" decides to lighten things up a bit. Maybe I'll be inspired by something I've read in the newspaper. Or maybe lightning will strike as I eavesdrop in a coffee shop (yes, I do that, so beware!), or while having an unexpected conversation with the cashier at the grocery store. I gather up the stuff some people say and do and let those elements roll around in my head.

Sometimes, however, the cause and effect is more direct. And more about me than you.

1. I hit a pothole and nearly break the axle of my car.

2. I get mad and swear (but it's not Tourette's).

3. Instead of calling City Hall to complain, I get out my pens and paper and begin sketching…

"WHAT REALLY GETS ME IS THAT OPPOSITE-SEX MARRIAGES HAVE ALWAYS BEEN LEGAL AND, STILL, STAN WON'T PROPOSE."

"DUDE, MAYBE WE'VE BEEN SMOKING TOO MUCH WEED..."

"LOOKS LIKE I'LL HAVE TO PRESCRIBE A CHOLESTEROL-LOWERING DRUG...
THE GOOD NEWS, THOUGH, IS THAT YOU QUIT SMOKING..."

"I KNEW IT WAS ONLY A MATTER OF TIME BEFORE
THEY RELOCATED THE AIRPORT CHECKPOINTS."

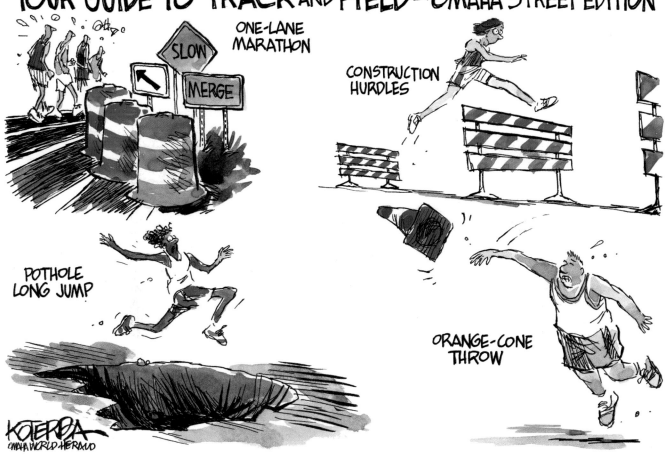

1992 JEFF KOTERBA
Form 1040P (Procrastinator)
Schedule
Part VI
Filing Status
Single (see page
Married, filing jointly
Married, filing Last-Minute
If Married, did your spouse ask you several times back in January to get an early start on this form?
Yes No
Did dependents nag you, too?
If so, their names & and ages
I NEVER SHOULD'VE WAITED...
While filling out this form, have you been using language not suitable for your dependents? Yes No
If yes, file form B-224-88
Part II
Attach Copy B of your form W-2 here.
If W-2 form lost in pile of "important papers" see schedule T-82
You Did hang on to your W-2 form, didn't you?
Did you learn your lesson this year? Yes No
Part III Will you be rushing off to your post office tonight?
Yes No
If so, Which one?
11th and Pacific, Omaha
If Mailing after 10 p.m. file schedule L-37
If line at post office longer than two blocks, see schedule S-484
How many dependents will be with you in your auto? Enter names on form Z7
While at post office, will you be voting for Elvis stamp?

All the President's Features

I KNOW A FEW cartoonists who revel in making fun of how politicians look. They go to such extremes as to make the person look ugly. For me, however, it's all about pointing out hypocrisy and irony. People — even well-known newsmakers — can't help how they look (well, OK, maybe Donald Trump could do something about that hair).

On the other hand, there's no better shorthand in a political cartoon than a good caricature. And what is a caricature if not an exaggerated depiction of someone's face? The more recognizable the politician, the better for me. But that also makes it more challenging. After all, everyone knows what the president looks like, and if I can't draw him for his one or two terms in office, well, then I'm really in trouble.

So I start with the eyes — they are the windows to the political soul, right? — and move on to the other features that stand out. George W. Bush's beady eyes. Clinton's bulbous nose. And, of course, Obama's ears. I latch onto all the easily recognizable features that will instantly tell the reader who it is. But again, there's a balance. If I take the caricature too far, the message might be lost. Still, a political cartoonist can have a little fun …

A Few More Lines

I never was very good at math, but by my own estimation, I've drawn more than 7,200 cartoons for The World-Herald. I also wasn't very good at deciding which cartoons to keep for this book and which to leave on the drawing room floor. So here are a few drawings that didn't make the original final cut and yet I just didn't have the heart to cast aside. Maybe it's the look on the faces of innocent children who are watching "WAR," or the ones who are starving on the street corner, that tug at my heartstrings. Likewise, the expression on Uncle Sam's face as he reacts to the slaying of journalist Daniel Pearl, the shape of Pearl's lifeless body formed from a news story about his horrific death.

In at least one case, my reason is personal: My father performed as a drummer with guitar legend Les Paul. I will admit, some cartoons still give me a chuckle — the arches on the Archway and Karl Rover running through George Bush's legs. And there are others I am drawn to for reasons I can't quite explain. The simplicity of President Obama's red line turned into a jump rope. The elegance of Tom Osborne's fishing line, cut by Dave Heineman's scissors. The details of bone and garbage in the drawing of Madeleine Albright in the dungeon.

While I have none of my cartoons on the walls at home, some keep me coming back time and again.

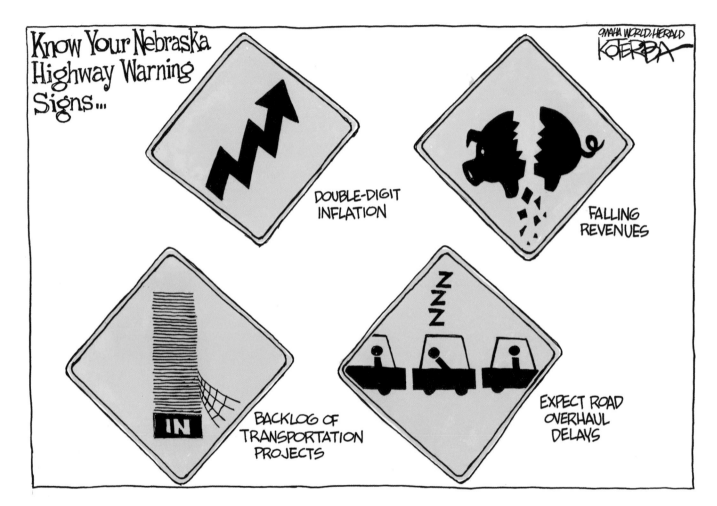

LES PAUL

THE INNOVATOR

KOTERBA
OMAHA WORLD-HERALD

"I DUNNO... MUST BE SOME NEW REALITY SHOW."

The VISIONARY and the OPPORTUNIST

SNIP

OSBORNE

HEINEMAN

KOTERBA
OMAHA WORLD-HERALD

ANOTHER WAY THE KEARNEY MONUMENT COULD TURN THINGS AROUND...

ARCHWAY TO ARCHES

KOTERBA
OMAHA WORLD-HERALD

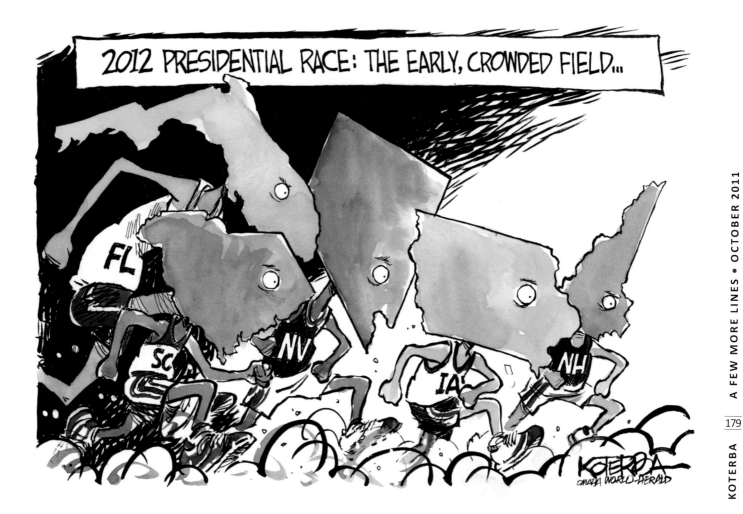

2012 PRESIDENTIAL RACE: THE EARLY, CROWDED FIELD...

OMAHA WORLD-HERALD
KOTERBA

WELCOME TO THE
UNITED STATES
OF GUNMERICA...

Acknowledgments

I AM BLESSED BEYOND BELIEF with loving friends and supportive family members, the list of which could fill an entire book. For his limitless patience, support, inspiration and keen, critical thinking, I am indebted to Josh Koterba. Hugs to Jennifer, Jonah and Juliet for helping me keep everything in perspective. Also to my mother, Helen, and siblings Artie, Jennifer, Eddie and Jeanie. Thank you to Liz Hruska, Clay Anderson, Kevin Quinn, Bruce Arant, Jason Levering, Amy Moore-Benson, Lori Young, Trilety Wade, Dana Altman, Dana Barfield, Bill Johnson, Jeff Beiermann, Howard K. Marcus, Mike Kelly, Mike Drelicharz, Josh Friedman and Chris Machian. My sincerest gratitude to Heidi Lang.

Making cartoons is a solitary endeavor. But if not for the expertise and generosity of World-Herald colleagues, past and present, it's difficult to imagine making all of the deadlines over the last 25 years. In no particular order, thank you to: Frank Partsch, Mike Holmes, Terry Kroeger, Larry King, Mike Reilly, Harold Andersen, John Gottschalk, Geitner Simmons, Aaron Sanderford, Jim Anderson, Ginny Bensheimer, John Malnack, Jolene McHugh and Bob Zurek. I also can't forget the incredible World-Herald library staff. Thank you to Marc Longbrake for the photo on the back cover. Not to mention the dedicated and talented team who put this book together, Christine Zueck-Watkins and Dan Sullivan.

Last, but not least, thank you to loyal readers of my cartoons — and, yes, even those who don't always agree with me.

About Jeff Koterba

JEFF KOTERBA BEGAN WORK at The World-Herald in 1989 and has since drawn more than 7,200 cartoons. His cartoons are popular features with readers of the newspaper and Omaha.com, and they are distributed to 400 papers nationwide. He graduated from Omaha South High and majored in art and journalism at the University of Nebraska at Omaha, where he won the Mark of Excellence Award for the nation's best college cartoonist. Koterba has been a finalist for Editorial Cartoonist of the Year from the National Cartoonists Society. He won first place for editorial cartooning in the Great Plains Journalism Awards in 2009, 2010 and 2013 and placed second in the National Headliner Awards in 2000 and 2012. He is the author of "Inklings," his memoir of growing up with Tourette's syndrome — defined by involuntary gestures such as sudden rapid movement, repeated vocalized sounds and twitches. It was named one of the best nonfiction books of 2009 by the Chicago Tribune. He also is a singer and musician who has performed with the Prairie Cats, a swing and jump-blues band that has appeared at the South by Southwest music festival.

EDITOR
DAN SULLIVAN

DESIGNER
CHRISTINE ZUECK-WATKINS

PHOTO IMAGING
JOLENE MCHUGH

CONTRIBUTING EDITORS
RICH MILLS
PAM THOMAS
PAM RICHTER
JIM ANDERSON
KATHY SULLIVAN

INTELLECTUAL PROPERTY MANAGER
MICHELLE GULLETT

PRINT AND PRODUCTION COORDINATORS
PAT "MURPHY" BENOIT
WAYNE HARTY

DIRECTOR OF MARKETING
RICH WARREN

EXECUTIVE EDITOR
MIKE REILLY

PRESIDENT AND PUBLISHER
TERRY KROEGER

Reprints of Jeff Koterba's cartoons are available from the OWHstore. Call 402-444-1014 to place an order or go to OWHstore.com.

AND FINALLY, A CARTOON THAT OFFENDS NO ONE...